Take My Hand

Hospice Volunteers
of Waldo County
PO Box 772
Belfast, ME 04915
(207) 338-3896

donated by
Ginny Rimn

Take My Hand

A Walk of Faith through Dark Places

Dan Cole

North Wind Publishing
Camden, Maine

North Wind Publishing
P.O. Box 192
Rockport, ME 04856
www.northwindpublishing.com

10 9 8 7 6 5 4 3 2 1

ISBN 0-9720620-0-9

Edited by Pamela Benner

Contents

Introduction

I SUPPOSE THERE MUST BE A REASON TO WRITE A BOOK. For Sandy and me it was initially a selfish way to invite people who care about us to join our journey into cancer treatment and prognosis. We had heard enough bad things about cancer to know it was a journey we could not face alone. I had presided at enough funerals to see the devastating effects it has on families. It seemed only reasonable that if we included friends in our journey, their company might make the experience more bearable.

In the summer of 2000 Sandy and I returned from working on the mission field in South Africa. It was time for a break, so we took the opportunity to visit churches all across the country to tell about our ministry there. The first six months were filled with speaking engagements, travel and folks who were eager to hear first-person stories about the hand of God at work in the developing world. We had included photos, movies, African art and African music. These made the congregants feel like an extension of our work. After all, they were responsible (in part) for our being there.

Halfway through our home assignment, however, something appeared to be wrong. Sandy was having trouble with her right hip. We laughed and attributed the pain to old age, even though she was only 57. But since I was already suffering from osteoarthritis, it seemed reasonable that she too might have an arthritic condition. We were living in the Chicago area and needed only to look in the phone book to find a doctor who specialized in bone conditions.

Our initial visit included an X-ray, which revealed some degeneration of the hipbone; in a few years the hip might need to be replaced. The doctor suggested physical therapy and a cane. So that was the route we took, but the therapy didn't give Sandy any relief, and after a few days she developed muscle cramps in her neck. We attributed this symptom to her shifting her weight while using the cane and to sleeping with too many pillows. Whatever the cause, it became clear that her symptoms were getting worse.

We returned to the doctor. This time he asked for a CAT scan, to look more carefully at the hip. It was then that he discovered a tumor about the size of Sandy's hand, wrapped around her hipbone. Next, we were referred directly to a bone cancer specialist at Rush Cancer Institute in Chicago, and he ordered a biopsy of the tissue to determine the cancer type. The results showed that Sandy had a large-cell soft-tissue cancer. This meant that the cancer had originated not in the hip, but in her soft tissues. A physician who specializes in this type of cancer would ultimately determine her treatment and prognosis.

The following pages include messages we sent to our friends and family over a seven-month period in an attempt to keep them not only informed, but also holding on with us as we faced this terrible enemy.

DAN COLE
2002

The Enemy

———

DEAR FRIENDS,

I sometimes worry that I am giving you too much information too fast. But fast is how these events are happening to us. I know that many of you are as anxious as we are for the next word in Sandy's progress. In a real sense, we have reached the end of one phase of the process. Today we met with the chief oncologist who is managing Sandy's case. The hunt for the primary cancer site is over, and all of the tests to discover the extent of her condition have been completed.

The diagnosis is stage-four lung cancer. The secondary sites are one in the left brain lobe, one at the base of the spine and the large one on her right hip. This is hardly the news we wanted to hear. Yesterday Sandy received medication to help restore her appetite. It has made a wonderful difference. Our three children have spent the past two days with us, and that has also been a great help.

The next few months will be filled with treatments and daily trips to the hospital. No one expects anything but improvement from this point. I print off every e-mail message you send so Sandy can read them all and be encouraged by your support. I will try to continue answering those of you who have questions.

Be assured that God has given us strength, friends, good medical resources and a powerful love that is woven into all of these. Sandy has found strength in God's word every day. For both of us, just knowing the name of the enemy and its location has given us reason to celebrate as we now plan the strategies for winning back her health. Pray for a good appetite, relief of pain and a plan of treatment that will arrest the spread of the cancer.

Please accept our humble thanks for your wonderful support.

Dan and Sandy

Radiation

DEAR FRIENDS,

Sandy has had some difficulty adjusting to the radiation, morphine and steroids, and for the past two days she has not been able to keep food down. Each day we rise and get ready to go to the hospital for the daily radiation treatment with confidence that the difficult path we are walking will continue to open doors for us to speak to others about our faith. Our daily routines are becoming increasingly time consuming. I told Sandy today that if she was looking to me for help with her makeup she might end up looking like Phyllis Diller or Mimi Carey.

Our time in the waiting room is usually spent in conversation with others who are there for radiation and facing similar struggles. What a place for ministry. Today Sandy was trying to finish her devotional time. She glanced up with a teary-eyed look and asked me to read the passage God gave her for this day.

Even to your old age and gray hairs I am HE, I am he who will sustain you. I have made you and I will carry you; I will sustain you and I will rescue you (Isaiah 46:4; NIV).

What an awesome God we serve to give us such great encouragement.

Dan and Sandy

Waiting-Room Blues

DEAR FRIENDS,

I am bringing you another chapter in our adventures with lung cancer, doctors, hospital waiting rooms, medication and the like. Over the past month I have tried to find a variety of ways to report to you the happenings in our lives. I trust that you will be able to sense the power of God at work and the emotional strength we feel, which we attribute in no small part to your faithful prayer support. Before I report on Sandy, I want to give you a sense of what it is like to travel to a downtown Chicago hospital each weekday for three weeks.

Unless you are familiar with the big-city flow of traffic that moves like the ocean's tide into the city in the morning and out of the city in the evening, our travels will have little meaning. We have been a part of that flow for fifteen days now. Upon arriving at the hospital, we have to deal with many departments and many doctors. There are X-rays, CAT scans, MRIs, blood work, oncologists, bone specialists, registration desks, nurses, doctors' assistants, fellows (understudy doctors) and the occasional person who is kind enough to give us directions as we roam the corridors looking for the site of our next appointment. I should also mention that at every stop we have to register again, filling out nearly identical forms, insurance information, a list of allergies, past ailments and personal stuff we weren't sure we wanted the receptionist to know.

I realize that I will probably not get a trophy, a plaque or even a certificate for hours spent in waiting rooms; however, I imagined that I might be issued some kind of card that could be punched for every five hours spent in a waiting-room chair. When all of the punches had been made, I would be entitled to return to the waiting room of my choice to spend the whole day . . . to sit . . . for no reason at all.

I have read every ratty issue of every old magazine in seven or eight waiting rooms at Rush Cancer Institute. The women's magazines are ripped to shreds. People have removed recipes, diets, love articles and gossip news until what is left looks very much like the Sears catalog in my grandmother's outhouse. The only pristine publication I found was *Bow and Arrow* from August of two years ago. I feel like writing a country western song called "The Waiting-Room Blues."

Dan and Sandy

My Wife . . . My Mentor

DEAR FRIENDS,

My silence is not for lack of things to say, but rather it is in awesome wonder of how God is leading us in this journey. I sometimes want to express things in terms of "good news" and "bad news." This past week produced both.

The good news is that Sandy's spirits are high and her emotional energy is buoyant. Her ability to minister to others during this time continually amazes me. It seems that this cancer has brought people closer to her, and she is somehow able to touch them with God's love. This week we made our first venture away from our apartment for an overnight trip to the St. Louis area. It was a test of sorts, to see how well she could travel and how stressful a trip might be for her. Apart from being tired, she did remarkably well.

But there was also bad news this week. Sandy's stepmother in Alabama passed away. It was very difficult to know that she could not attend the funeral or stand by her elderly father in this time of grief. As an only child, she found it painful to call her dad and explain her love for him but without being in his presence.

Many of you have asked about me, and I appreciate your concern. I don't think I ever considered how I might behave if I were in Sandy's shoes. But she has taught me so much about the joy of life, abiding faith and a complete openness about all she is experiencing. I now know that I want to be just like her. Even books are not helpful for some things in life (like raising kids and facing powerful enemies like cancer), but if a person finds a mentor, then he/she is truly blessed. I have found my mentor.

We are still walking together.

Dan and Sandy

Breaths of Prayer

DEAR FRIENDS,

As you wait for updates on Sandy's struggle, you may rejoice with us that she has felt well enough to travel. We have been taking short trips, and she has tolerated the travel and finds energy to interact with those we visit. We will leave this weekend for a trip to Alabama to visit her dad, who lost his wife a couple of weeks ago. This is Sandy's best window of opportunity. I am glad to give a good report of renewed strength. To see her standing and walking with a cane is a wonderful testimony of her fortitude, positive attitude and spiritual strength—all nourished by the prayers of so many. Chemotherapy begins in a week and a half. I am sure that new challenges lie ahead.

We thank God for your prayers, your kind words and your encouragement. We often think of prayer as a specific time we set aside for having conversation with God. Yet when friends are as close as we have been during a crisis, it is not necessary to make time to pray for each other as we might normally do. Prayer for each other is within each breath that we take and part of the wandering of the mind that finds its resting place on those we love.

Dan and Sandy

Do Not Give Up

DEAR FRIENDS,

Your faithfulness in prayer, Sandy's determination and God's grace have brought us far. This past week we took a trip to Tennessee and Alabama. It was time for Sandy to reunite with her dad and bring closure to the death of his wife. Because of Sandy's condition, she was not able to travel to attend the funeral three weeks ago. However, her improvement has allowed Sandy to make this important trip, which she endured well. We arrived home tired but thankful for the time spent with family. During this past week Sandy has been able to leave the wheelchair behind and walk with a cane. She has also successfully eliminated the morphine and is managing her pain with Celebrex® and Aleve®.

Today's trip to the hospital included a CAT scan, blood tests and a consultation with the oncologist. The size of the known tumors has been reduced by the radiation treatments. There are two small tumors that have appeared since the last scan. These additional tumors were expected and are considered a normal occurrence at this stage of cancer treatment. The doctor was not particularly concerned because the chemotherapy, which starts on Wednesday, will address this problem.

Amazingly, the tumor on her lung—the source of her cancer—has actually shrunk! The doctor was amazed because this type of tumor normally increases in size, and nothing the medical staff has done can account for the reduction. We are confident that the fervent prayers of the righteous avail much.

We have done a great deal of research on both conventional and unconventional treatments for Sandy's type of cancer and discussed these options at length with the oncologist. We are confident that the multidisciplinary approach we have chosen is right for us. Our treatment plan consists of a healthy diet with an emphasis on vegetables and fruit, plenty of rest, day-to-day support from family and friends, confidence in the competency of our doctors and other caregivers, positive attitudes, trust in the Lord and the powerful prayer support of folks like you. It is both a wonderful privilege and a great responsibility to know that we are included in the process and plan for our own wellness and future. I suppose when you think about it, each of us makes those decisions every day. Please know that your partnership in this process is an important part of the good news we report today. Let me leave you with this note of encouragement from Paul's letter to the church at Galatia.

> *Let us not become weary in doing good, for*
> *at the proper time we will reap a harvest if we*
> ***do not give up*** *(Galatians 6:9; NIV).*

Thanks for not giving up.

Dan and Sandy

More Waiting-Room Blues

DEAR FRIENDS,

If you need to make a telephone call you can use the phone provided in each waiting room. It is a convenience made available for those who must spend the day in the hospital's waiting rooms. In one instance we waited for three hours for our name to be called. I began to fantasize about using the phone to call the psychic hot line, desperately wanting someone to tell me if we would see the doctor that day.

I had become so bored at one point that I caught myself staring at the freckles on my arm. I took out my pen and started to connect the dots but then I realized what I was doing. I wonder if anyone has ever written a book on survival tactics for the hospital waiting room? To my joy, we finally did get to see the doctor that day.

At home I sorted through the different medications that Sandy takes at different times of the day. Some require food first, while others must be taken before you eat. One has to be taken an hour before any of the others to prevent the rest from coming back up. I bought one of those plastic pillboxes with thirty compartments for five time periods each day of the week. I sat at the table with each bottle in hand, trying to figure out which pill to put into which compartment. The medication that requires varying dosages was the worst: three tablets for the first four days, two for the next four days, one for the next four days, and then I had to break the tiny pill in half for the final four days. Pill time became a game as Sandy tried to recognize which pill she was taking and for what symptom. I am now confident that one of life's greatest fears as we age is "medication management."

Today Sandy received good news. She will not have to undergo more radiation; she will be weaned from the steroids and the morphine; and she will not have to return to the hospital for one month while her body recovers from the previous treatments and medication. In one month she will begin her chemotherapy: one day a week for three weeks, one week off and then back on for another three weeks. The number of cycles will be determined by Sandy's response to the treatment and its effectiveness in arresting the cancer.

This Easter we are celebrating with you that the risen Lord is the Lord of new life indeed.

Dan and Sandy

Songs in the Darkness

DEAR FRIENDS,

The thing about moving through the valley of the shadow of death is that you cannot tell the shadows from the real danger. This phenomenon makes a person edgy; one wonders if what one faces today is just part of the journey or part of the disaster.

So where do the prayers of so many of you fit into this picture? Well, to us those prayers are like the birds singing in the trees about us. We cannot see most of you, yet we have heard from many of you. And we can sense the impact of all of you. That singing in the darkness reminds us that all is well. It reminds us that the one who wrote of a "valley of the shadow of death" (Psalm 23:4; NIV) also wrote "I will lift up mine eyes unto the hills, from whence cometh my help. My help cometh from the LORD, which made heaven and earth" as well as the valleys and the hills (Psalm 121:1–2; KJV).

It is difficult for us to describe the impact that your faithfulness is having on our lives. Through your prayers you are singing the song of heaven. None of you have all of the words. None of you have the whole melody. None of you can produce all of the harmony. Yet all together you produce extraordinary music before the Lord, which I am sure is pleasing to him.

Sandy had her first chemotherapy treatment yesterday. Though it took four hours and several bags of fluid, she had NO adverse reaction to the chemicals. Praise the Lord! She will return for one day a week for two more weeks and then get a week off. We are indeed excited. Even as I write these words, a robin is singing loudly outside my window.

As you take this journey with us, may each of you receive the reward that God has prepared for you.

We are the benefactors of heavenly music.

Dan and Sandy

Is This Normal?

DEAR FRIENDS,

I have delayed writing so I could report the results of Sandy's first cycle of chemotherapy. There is a sort of paranoia that comes with having cancer. If you get a new ache, or nausea, or something appears that you can't identify, or sleep escapes you, or even if you seem to sleep more than normal, you find yourself wondering how this is related to the cancer. Then of course there are the side effects from the radiation and chemotherapy to consider. And let's not forget the drugs given to counteract effects such as nausea, pain and digestive turmoil. Through all of this, it becomes difficult to remember what is "normal." But even as the most skilled doctors attempt to act on and to counteract what is happening to Sandy in the elusive attempt to find "normal," I am reminded how wonderfully made we are and how so much happens to keep us "normal" every day, automatically, as God designed it to be.

Psalm 139:14–18 (NIV)

14 I praise you because I am fearfully and wonderfully made; your works are wonderful, I know that full well.

15 My frame was not hidden from you when I was made in the secret place. When I was woven

together in the depths of the earth, 16 your eyes saw my unformed body. All the days ordained for me were written in your book before one of them came to be.

17 How precious to me are your thoughts, O God! How vast is the sum of them!

18 Were I to count them, they would outnumber the grains of sand. When I awake, I am still with you.

Weakened by nausea, Sandy took her third dose of Taxol® (one of the chemicals used in the treatment) last week. She also needed to get the dosage of steroid adjusted. As a result, her appetite has returned, as has her strength. She was strong enough to insist on making an appearance at a women's mission meeting in Indiana while visiting with our daughter. This week is her week without chemotherapy, and she is using it to build her strength. Next week we will leave for Providence, Rhode Island, to attend the national American Baptist Biennial. With our meager resources and knowledge, we deal with Sandy's complex health issues and find ourselves amazed that there are days of victory. I am confident that each of you, through your prayers and encouragement, is an important part of the mystery that is keeping Sandy struggling toward "normal."

We are humbled to know that with limited knowledge and resources mankind can "tinker" with the body (God's creation) in an effort to stay alive. Even though we are not seeking perfection, we struggle to hold on to what is *normal*.

Dan and Sandy

Manna for the Moment

Dear Friends,

There is a Bible story in the Book of Exodus of how God provided for the daily needs of his people. God supplied just enough food for that day. On the next day a new supply was given. This provision was called manna. Manna has come to symbolize God's daily provision for those he loves. (Exodus 16:1–36; NIV).

Just when you thought that it might be time to turn your attention to other prayer needs, this note comes as a reminder that God continues to work in our lives. It seems that each day contains new information about the complex mysteries of our health. This past week reminded me that I often have no clue as to how our future will unfold. Yet with confidence we continue to trust in the one who has a plan for each of us. We are not unlike others who daily rely on the Lord for "manna for the moment."

Last week I decided to do something about a lump that was growing in my neck. It had reached the size of a golf ball and was pressing into my throat. The doctor advised surgery, so on Tuesday I had the mass removed. On Wednesday I spoke to the surgeon about the nature of the growth. He said that he could not identify the mass but had sent it off for a biopsy. Jokingly I suggested that it might be a colony of African ants. Truth be known, I needed "manna for the moment."

On the day that the anesthetic was wearing off, we were packing for our trip to the biennial meeting in Rhode Island. On Thursday we boarded the plane (without Sandy's wheelchair)—I with a large patch on my throat and Sandy with cane in hand. By this time we were both needing "manna for the moment."

On Friday my head was clear, my neck was sore and my attention again returned to Sandy and her needs. Sandy had been invited to be the plenary speaker at the women's luncheon. More than 700 women were expected to attend. This was a very important moment in Sandy's life. She would finally meet women from all over the country who had been praying for her and encouraging her in her ministry. There seemed to be lots of last-minute details, including transportation and assistance, should she need it. People were wonderfully attentive, yet I knew that she needed "manna for the moment."

We returned home having had a wonderful experience. But the euphoria was short-lived. At the hospital Sandy faced another round of chemotherapy. Blood tests revealed a low red-cell count. It was time for another wrinkle in Sandy's progress, and she needed additional "manna for the moment."

I went to the doctor's office today to have the stitches removed and to get the results of the pathology report. The scar is healing well; however, the pathology report reads: Burkitt or Burkitt-type lymphoma. My heart sank as I heard those words. Now I too am in need of "manna for the moment."

Dan and Sandy

Jesus Is Coming

———

DEAR FRIENDS,

Today is the third day in a row that we have been at the hospital for tests. This was Sandy's midway milestone for her chemotherapy. She had a CAT scan to evaluate her progress, and then she was scheduled to have a doctor's appointment to begin her third round of treatments. The doctor was out of the office, though, so her appointment was rescheduled for tomorrow.

Having a free afternoon was a gift to us. So we took advantage of this gift of time by running errands and eating lunch. When we arrived back at the apartment, there was a message on the phone from the hospital. The scan had revealed some unexpected news. A call to the nurse indicated blood clots in Sandy's lungs and an infection. We were to go to the emergency room, where she would be checked into the hospital.

The emergency room was jammed with people. A woman had fainted on the street. A child had a broken arm. Several police-academy students were injured. We heard coughing, wheezing, crying and angry voices barking at the very people who were trying to help those who were angry. It took a while for a nurse and doctor to check on Sandy. I am always amazed that in the midst of such chaos, there are angels of love who gently and lovingly work to restore order.

The hospital beds that had staff to oversee them were all taken. So we would wait. The IV was started, blood samples taken and a heart monitor connected. So we waited, listening to the commotion and chasing images of the television version of ER. And we waited. . . .

After several hours a nurse came by and said, "I have good news. We have a place for you. Jesus is coming to take you in a few minutes." Her words took us by surprise. We were caught between two emotional planes. On the one hand, the coming of Jesus is something understood by many as the hope and expectation of all of those who love the Lord. On the other hand, we had not anticipated that it would happen this way. We had hoped for trumpets, a splitting sky or something a bit more dramatic, not a nurse's matter-of-fact announcement.

Shortly thereafter, a young man wearing a hospital tag that said "Jesus" arrived to take Sandy to her room. Sandy will remain in Rush Cancer Institute for a few days for treatment of the blood clots. Tomorrow I will see my oncologist and probably start my chemotherapy.

Perhaps the words "Jesus is coming" are just the words we needed to hear. They remind us that there is one who is concerned about our struggle and wants to enter the chaos that now fills our lives.

Dan and Sandy

A New Mission Field

DEAR FRIENDS,

I have been teaching and practicing "missions" most of my adult life. For example, I am well aware of the influence that Constantine, the Roman emperor, has had on our thought that missions is beyond our borders. I am equally aware of the more contemporary emphasis on missions that points us to those around us. This weekend I learned of a new mission field that I had not considered and which is neither of these.

A church in our region brought their youth to the Chicago area for a mission experience. One of their stops on Saturday evening was the Northern Seminary, where they would meet the missionaries from South Africa (us). At the same time (and unknown to the youth group) a missionary friend from Central America was scheduled to visit us for a couple of days and would be available to add another dimension to the mission story. I enjoy sharing with teens the passion of missions. They almost always ask, "What can I do?" This gives me a chance to talk about where they will find their mission field.

Friday afternoon I hurried home from Rush to meet our missionary friend. It was wonderful to see her again. I told her what was happening to us, and she wanted to go immediately back to the hospital to see Sandy. There seemed little time for "shop" talk, as we had so much recent personal history to share.

We arrived at the hospital with a couple of hours left on the normal visitors' schedule. Then something unexpected happened. I was standing off to the side of the room while Sandy was catching up on hugs and family issues. As if someone had crept up behind me, I felt what seemed like a knife stabbing me in the lower left flank. I instantly broke out in a sweat and grabbed my side. Within a few seconds I was overtaken by nausea. Sandy and our missionary friend rushed to my side and helped me to a chair in the rest room. I knew that I was close to passing out. Sandy called for the nurse; she took my vitals and surmised that I was struggling with a kidney stone. There was little else to do but head to the emergency room. A call was sent out for a wheelchair to take me away.

The journey from the eleventh floor to the emergency room made the hospital seem bigger than ever. Sandy grabbed a robe and the hand of our friend and both came along. I am sure we were quite a sight sitting in the chairs in the waiting room— Sandy in a robe with an IV in her arm, our friend who had no idea what she had gotten herself into and me wrenching with pain. In short order we found our way to an exam room. Thank the Lord the waiting room was not chaotic, as it had been a few days prior when Sandy was admitted. As I lay on the gurney, the pain subsided and my life seemed to come back to me. We were already checked in, however, and to get checked out would involve an exam by the doctor. Everyone could see that I had improved remarkably. Sandy and our visitor went back to Sandy's room. I would follow as soon as I could get signed out.

About twenty minutes later, I made my way back to Sandy's room. By this time it was 9 P.M. and our friend and I had missed our supper. The missionary and I said our good nights and headed to the elevator. We stepped inside, the doors closed and it happened again. This time that "knife" was plunged deep into my back, and I grabbed for the walls of the elevator to keep from falling. You guessed it, we headed straight for the emergency room again.

Onto the gurney . . . in went the IV . . . next came the morphine. Within a few minutes the pain was easing. I remained in the emergency room for the rest of the night. Except during CT scan and X-ray, our missionary friend sat by my side in a hard plastic chair for eleven hours, until 8 A.M. the next day. She made the entire difficult journey with me.

The doctor found the stone, which was too large to pass. Removal of this stone will be one more thing added to the events of our lives this week.

A few days after this emergency-room experience I reflected on the impact it had had on my life. Today I was reading the Book of James. The passage I read suggested that we should count our difficult circumstances as joy because of what they can do for us spiritually. Then it dawned on me: here was a missionary sent to another country and culture, one who could clearly define her mission field. But for one night, in a strange place and under difficult circumstances, she found a new mission field. That mission field was *me*.

Missions is about giving *and* receiving. Perhaps I too needed to learn what the apostle Peter learned by having his feet washed. Before you give kindness (in missions) you may need to learn how to receive it.

Just another note from our mission field to yours,

Dan and Sandy

From the Foot of the Hill

DEAR FRIENDS,

Help is an odd little four-letter word. Perhaps this is because it is an expression of extremes. One person cries "HELP" out of desperation, while another expresses confidence with, "I can help myself." *Help* is the word we use to express the condition we feel when something is just beyond our reach. There are some who are always crying for help. There are others who wait too long before they admit that they need help. It seems that when and where we look for help can make all the difference in the world. This is another of the lessons we have revisited during our present struggle. Where will we go to find help for all that is going on in our lives? Cancer, kidney stones, chemotherapy, to say nothing of the emotional impact; there are so many reasons to cry out for help. The Psalm writer said that he lifted up his eyes to the hills and asked the all-important question, "Where is *my* help coming from?" (Psalm 121; NIV).

As a boy I played a game with my friends. When we found a pile of dirt, one person stood on top and declared himself King of the Hill. If anyone else wanted to be king, he had to attempt (one at a time) to pull the king off the hill. Whoever succeeded was declared the new king. What I have discovered with age is that adults play the same game. The only things that have changed in the game are the hills. Somehow, all of us admire those who get to the top. Since most of us will never make it, we look for help to those who do. Hills evoke the high ground, a place of advantage where a person has the power to change things. This is what the military teaches. This kind of help appeals especially to those of us who believe we are disadvantaged. Almost bigger than life, the doctors, nurses and medical personnel stand over Sandy and me on the hill called medicine. Those at the bottom of the hill are looking to those on top of the hill for help.

A simple question has guided us in our search for help during this present struggle. *What do you have when you get what you want?*

Eve wanted the fruit placed just out of her reach (Genesis 3). Lot wanted the green valley that lay near Sodom, just beyond his reach and out of his uncle Abram's control (Genesis 13). David wanted Bathsheba, just beyond his reach in Uriah's house (2 Samuel 11). When you and I look for help, it makes a big difference where we look. For out of our desire, the thing we appear to want may not be what we want at all. Real help does not come from the desire of our soul, from solutions to health issues, from someone's power or cleverness or from being in a place of advantage. Real help comes from the one who makes the hills. The secret to finding help is in finding the desires of the heart of the Hill Maker.

Earlier last week I had a very unpleasant ordeal at the hospital during treatment for my kidney stone. The procedures caused more pain than I want to confess. Two days later I had surgery to implant a device beneath the skin, used to access veins. This devise allows the medical staff to administer chemotherapy and other medications intravenously. THEN came chemotherapy for both of us. "Help" didn't quite encompass all that went through my mind, but "help" was a big part of it. Our testimony is that we did find help, and it came from the one who makes hills, and kidneys, and hearts, and hips and all the other parts of us. He knows the very working of our inner being, knows our needs and hears our cries for help. When we call for help out of our desperate condition, and when our eyes are able to see beyond our problems, even beyond the hills of temporary hope, just out of our reach, it is there that we will find the Hill Maker.

The Lord will watch over your coming
and going both now and forevermore
(Psalm 121:8; NIV).

Still on the journey, receiving God's wonderful grace
and the encouragement of your love.

Dan and Sandy

Overwhelmed

DEAR FRIENDS,

What does it mean to you to be overwhelmed? As a pastor and counselor for many years, I have encountered my fair share of people who have been overwhelmed and in distress. But I'll be honest with you: After hearing many of their stories of busy schedules, impossible demands and bills, I wanted to say, "DUH! What did you expect with that kind of behavior?"

On the other hand, there were others who, because of things beyond their control—such as lost jobs, illness and death—were genuinely overwhelmed. Over the years Sandy and I have tried to distinguish between the two conditions and not add to the list of things that sooner or later will overwhelm each of us.

This past week Sandy and I experienced an energy shortage. Today our fatigue came into sharp focus. Neither of us had the energy to walk to another part of the campus to get the mail or to do the laundry or to clean the apartment. We showered, ate some breakfast, and took our medication. That's it! We were out of energy and feeling overwhelmed by tasks that are normally added to the stride of our day. Helplessness descended upon us. With blank, hollow looks on our faces, we stood speechless in front of a pile of laundry.

In moments like these our hearts turn to the Lord who has been our strength in times of weakness. But today we were so overwhelmed, neither of us knew what to say. Would God even care about our dirty apartment or laundry? Our silence was broken by a knock on the door. A young African-American student who calls us Mom and Dad stood there asking what he could do for us today. We thanked him and sent him off to the administration building to pick up our mail and add money to our laundry account. He walked away, and Sandy closed the door. We stared at each other in disbelief. Within seconds the phone rang. It was a young mother of two small boys who lives in our building. She wanted to do our laundry and stop by later in the week to clean our apartment. Sandy hung up the phone and related the conversation. I don't think I can describe the look on our faces then. Somehow, in less than five minutes, the distress of being overwhelmed had disappeared and was replaced with wonderment.

Today our world contains two kinds of people: those who are overwhelmed and those who respond to the prompting of God to transform someone else's distress into wonderment. After all, isn't it the Spirit within us that helps us in our weakness? When we do not know how to pray, it is the Spirit who is already speaking to God in a way we do not understand (Romans 8:26–27).

As strange as this may sound to some, it is in our weakness that our faith has made us more than conquerors of this day.

Dan and Sandy

Sharing Burdens

Dear Friends,

You have been so faithful to walk with us in this struggle. Many have written or called or visited, and so many more are praying for us as these notes are shared with others. We are well aware of the powerful effect you are having in our lives and how this journey together has become a ministry to many.

Let me begin with the burdens of these past few days. Sandy and I were both scheduled to have our chemo treatments this week. Our daughter and son were here to help us with transportation and the daily stuff of survival. By the way, God has blessed us with great, loving children. When we arrived, the hospital staff discovered that Sandy was too anemic to be treated. Instead she would get two units of blood the next day, and her treatments were postponed. Her X-rays showed the cancer in her lung to be nearly gone. I went to get checked out, and my blood pressure was 70 over 50. I was extremely dehydrated and the nurse was surprised that I could stand. After they gave me some fluids, my blood pressure returned to normal, and I was able to take my treatment. Both of us have had low energy these past few days.

Now permit me to address the importance of sharing burdens. Some of you have written to share burdens of your own and simultaneously apologized (as if you didn't want to add to our burdens). You cannot know how important they are to us. Perhaps this small story from my own childhood will help.

When I was 10 years old I lived on a small farm in Tennessee. My grandfather came one day to help my dad with his work. Granddad and I were to begin the day by feeding the pigs. We went to the barn where there were four large buckets, which we loaded full of corn. They were heavy. Granddad picked up two of them and told me to pick up the other two. I tried to lift one and could barely get it off the ground. I pulled it with both arms until the top of the bucket touched my knees. I was doubled over, straining and dragging it across my legs to walk. Granddad barked at me and told me to put the bucket down. He then instructed me to stand between the buckets, bend over and pick up one in each hand and to stand by using the muscles in my legs for strength. To my amazement I was able to carry two buckets more easily than one. The second bucket had given me balance.

It seems to me that we often are so consumed with our own burdens that we find ourselves doubled over in a deep struggle to survive. We move through the day wondering how we will make it. But God has given us the capacity to share our burdens with each other and thus restore balance to our lives and to the community of faith. The benefit of carrying someone else's burden while struggling with your own is that it makes your own struggle easier to bear. Keep in mind that real balance does not occur until the loads are equal. Those of you who have been brave enough to share your struggles with us have given us a great blessing.

> _Carry each other's burdens, and in this way_
> _you will fulfill the law of Christ_
> _(Galatians 6:2; NIV)._

Go ahead and pick up someone else's load. The blessing will belong to both of you.

Dan and Sandy, sharing our load

The Big Picture

DEAR FRIENDS,

Your response to our last e-mail was humbling. Many of you shared the struggles you are facing. We take this responsibility as a sacred trust. Sandy and I have started a prayer log that sits next to the computer so we can be reminded of every need. I only wish that time permitted us to respond personally to each of you who writes. By now there are hundreds of you in many countries receiving these updates. Many of you are responding, and we read all of your responses.

How often have you heard the words, "You must see the big picture"? First, let me give you our little picture. These past two weeks have been a time of transition for Sandy. She has stopped her chemotherapy and been given a series of tests to evaluate her progress. The CAT scans and MRI have revealed that many, but not all, of the tumors have shrunk. This has prompted her doctor to pull out of his arsenal a new regimen of chemicals. This series will extend her treatments to around Christmastime.

As for me, I am starting my third cycle (of six) of chemotherapy. My energy is returning, as I am tolerating the treatment better now than in the beginning. I recently fought off a bladder infection, and I still battle with kidney stones. We are rejoicing in our

newly found energy, which has allowed us to interact more with our world. Last weekend we took
time to visit family in Indianapolis. As we weave our
way through each day, we are tempted to see only
that day, only our own difficulty and only the thing
we cannot yet have. But there is a bigger picture. At
this point, I think a story about one of our kids is in
order.

When we once lived in a rural area, our kids
learned much about life from nature. On one occasion our daughter found a cocoon. She was anxious
to know what was inside. We explained that it was a
caterpillar and that it would one day emerge as a
butterfly. I am sure this did not seem possible to her.
She put it in a jar, hid it in her closet and occasion-
ally took it out to see what was happening. One day
it started to move. She lay on the floor for nearly an
hour, watching the cocoon twitch on the branch. But
nothing happened.

The next day she noticed that the cocoon had
split and she could see something inside. By this time
she had taken it out of the jar for closer inspection.
Her heart was filled with sympathy for the struggling
little creature that she knew was a butterfly. After
some time she grew impatient, reached down and
gently split away the cocoon to help the butterfly
emerge. What came out was a fat misshapen crea-

ture that was neither butterfly nor caterpillar. In a short time it died. What she didn't know was the big picture. Butterflies are born out of the struggle to emerge from their cocoons. It takes time to develop the wings, legs and other parts that give birth to a new creature.

So here we are, perhaps like many of you, caught in the small picture, struggling, believing that there is something on the other side of the struggle that is bigger than what we are facing today. It was true for Joseph, it was true for Job and it was true for Jesus.

> *Perseverance must finish its work*
> *so that you may be mature and*
> *complete, not lacking anything*
> *(James 1:4; NIV).*

Perhaps we can't understand the little picture until we understand the big picture.

Yet to emerge, and still in the struggle,

Dan and Sandy

We Are Changing

Dear Friends,

As I reflect on all that has happened to us in this past year, I suppose that the statement, "We are changing," seems obvious. With every passing day there is a new change in our bodies, our attitudes, our relationships and our understanding of the future.

This week I finished the third cycle of six cycles of chemotherapy treatments. In a sense, this is a milestone. Someone said that I must be glad to be halfway. I told him that what happened in the first half determines whether a person is ready to face the second half. My next cycle of chemotherapy will begin on Thursday of next week. On Tuesday, however, I will have the stint removed from my kidney and a CAT scan to check that no new tumors have formed.

Sandy, on the other hand, is not fairing well. She has been progressively short-winded, and her energy has decreased over the past week. She did take her chemotherapy treatment, and the doctor added oxygen to the list of things we must manage. Our apartment now has machines, bottles and gauges, tubes and filters, dials and switches—all of which we are learning to use. Sandy is feeling much worse.

After only one night of oxygen, Sandy could hardly breathe when she got up in the morning. So we made the trek to the emergency room. We are now able to call much of the staff by their first name. She was admitted to the hospital with what appears to be pneumonia and a nasty infection around the implant area where the IV is connected. She will remain in the hospital until these problems have cleared up. These are this week's changes in our lives.

After receiving a devotional note from a friend this week, Sandy and I reflected on the changes that have taken place in our lives. What things can we see in ourselves and in each other that are different because of this journey? Some of the things we knew but failed to practice. Others are things we did but not well. And still others are new territory for us.

Here is our list:

It matters little what others think.

There is a powerful effect on our lives when we know that we are REALLY loved.

We have learned to enjoy an entire day from sunrise to the closing of our eyes.

Tomorrow is not our problem.

Prayer comes easily—in a whisper—in a moment—in a tear.

We can talk about serious matters, seriously.

It helps to keep the big picture.

Carrying someone else's burden makes ours lighter.

Dealing with fear of the unknown requires faith, trust, hope and love. As fear begins to disappear, we discover the presence of God.

In confusion, frustration or haste we often overlook the obvious.

Crying is not only okay; it is better when it is shared.

Bald can be very beautiful.

Identifying the changes in our lives has helped us to affirm the good that is happening while we are struggling with things that are not so good. We will be different because of this experience, and perhaps we will continue to embrace changes that will take us to the end of our lives.

In the midst of transformation we remain,

Dan and Sandy

Take My Hand

DEAR FRIENDS,

The days are filled with ups and downs. Sandy's critical condition is stable, but she has spent the day struggling to get enough oxygen. With the help of medication, oxygen, the good work of a respiratory therapist and God's gift of another breath, she is managing much better. We received a wonderful blessing from the visits of missionary colleagues who are in the States on home assignment. Even the visits, however, are more than Sandy is able to manage at times.

As the day wound down, the doctor made his evening rounds. Soon after, Sandy reached up and said to me, "Take my hand."

As I reflected on this gesture, which has been part of our relationship for nearly forty years, I realized its great significance. One of the first things an infant does is to wave his or her little hands, reaching for someone to touch. By placing our fingers inside a baby's tiny palms, we introduce the child to a bonding touch that starts the journey of life.

Later we reach again to our babies and pull them to a standing position. Again we take a hand to guide them to walk, and marvel when they can do it without us. Yet we are thrilled when they reach for our hand, to cross the street or for a hug.

When a teen tentatively reaches to take the hand

of another teen, that same need for bonding is being expressed. When this gesture is met with the same gentle kindness once expressed by loving parents, something mystical happens. Before long there is a "giving of the hand" in marriage. It is a symbol of the touch that will last for the rest of a person's life. The strength of a marriage relationship can be measured by the practice of holding hands.

When life is at a critical point, some will return to the practice of holding hands (when this habit is not already part of the relationship). This act may have little meaning beyond an attempt to comfort, but for those of us who have experienced a lifetime of placing one hand inside another, it is boundless love, speechless wonder and inner peace.

What a thrill for me to hear the words, "Take my hand." There are no words that can replace those. There is nothing more valuable. There is nothing as simple and yet so binding from the altar to the grave than to hold the hand of the one who loves you.

You too can know what we know. To someone you love, or to someone who needs your love, say these three words, "Take my hand."

Holding on to each other,

Dan and Sandy

Worship

DEAR FRIENDS,

These days Sandy's battle with cancer is on selective grounds. That is, the doctor selects the tumor or condition that is causing the most trouble in sustaining life and makes that the focus. The tumor in her chest is pressing on her windpipe and cutting off her breathing. We agreed to try radiation in an attempt to stop the growth of this tumor. As I understand it, radiation affects the way cancer cells multiply in the second and third generations after the treatment. The race is on to see if the tumor will grow faster than the radiation can work, or whether the radiation will curb the growth and reverse the process. All of this means that we continue to live in the moment.

If a patient is confined to bed, Sunday is much like any other day. There are fewer tests, less staff and more visitors. Otherwise, there is little difference in the passing of the day. In these circumstances where does one find a place to worship? As I struggled with this need, my first thoughts of worship were, how? I reflected on some manner or form of worship that I had known (and led) all my life. Worship is another aspect of life that I sensed would change. We had no stained glass, no pews, no hymnals and no musical instruments. We had no bulletin to dictate the order of service, nor did we choose to read from the Bible. Nevertheless, worship happened anyway.

We did not ask God into our presence. Yet the God within us burst into our awareness as we turned ourselves toward him. God was present in our speech, in our tears and in our stories. True worship is not a product of the trappings around us.

The Scriptures, which had been hidden in our hearts, now echoed their timeless principles in our quivering voices. The oneness that we had so often prayed for and sometimes had known was expressed through our silence, during which our eyes spoke for us. It is uncanny that, without speaking, each of us knew what the other was saying. Our offerings were our lives laid upon an altar like living sacrifices, open and exposed to the Lord and to each other.

One Sunday our children arrived to join us in the intensive care unit. We focused on the impact that this illness was having on our family. Some of what needed to be said was spoken aloud. Much of it was not. Yet it was clear that we understood what was happening to each of us. Our songs of worship were the joys within us as memories of meaningful family gatherings flooded our minds and bathed our conversation. Our prayers became the binding together of our hearts before the Lord; we counted it a blessing to take this sacred journey together.

On a separate occasion, Sandy and I were alone. In this same spirit of worship, we spoke of what death would mean to each of us. It was so hard not to be selfish and feel trapped in the moment. In the midst of our painful discussion, the phone in Sandy's room rang. It was a friend of more that fifteen years who had lost a daughter in a recent auto accident. After wishing Sandy well and praying for her, she told Sandy that she knew that Sandy would likely see her daughter before she did. Would she please tell her that her mom loves her? When Sandy shared the conversation, we smiled. The Lord had reminded us that death is not an end but a passage. Some will make their passage while others remain behind. I couldn't resist telling her that I had a list of folks I wanted her to look up for me.

Perhaps all this seems like a strange form of worship. Or perhaps I have chosen a word that belongs in another setting. In either case, I have attempted to describe in a transparent way how our faith is guiding us through these difficult days. Though our faith is strong and our hope is sure, it is our love that sustains us for this moment.

Dan and Sandy

The End

Dear Friends,

This is the most difficult note to write. I arrived at the hospital early in the morning to find that my sister was already there. Sandy did not respond to my usual morning kiss and greeting. Her breathing was slow and shallow, not labored as it had been. I knew her life was coming to an end.

I sat by the side of her bed, holding her hand and telling her of the events that had transpired since the night before. Then I reached for the stack of e-mails that had arrived that morning so that I could read them to her. The first was from a Zulu pastor's wife who was praying for her. She was also reporting on the fall conference meeting of the churches of Kwa-Zulu Natal in South Africa. In the e-mail message she reported how effective Sandy's AIDS awareness work had been and how well the churches were responding to the messages she had taught them.

It seems as if Sandy had been waiting for that news. It was then that she took her last breath. I am confident that she gave everything within her to the children she held, the church leaders she counseled, and the friends she knew—all of whom had AIDS and are now with her in glory.

I could do little more than slump in my chair while still holding her hand. I felt as if my heart was being torn from my body. I have never known such pain. In many ways I am grateful for the seven months we had together from the time we got the report of the seriousness of her cancer. We did not waste those precious days. We spent hours holding hands and struggling with the death that was tearing us apart. It wasn't until sometime after Sandy's death that I realized how much she had helped me deal with issues I would face after she was gone. The funeral, the memorial service and even the loneliness I would face were all the final pieces to a partnership of nearly forty years.

I am comforted in the assurance that Sandy is at peace. Now my energy turns toward my own recovery. I have been so focused on Sandy during this journey we have taken together that I have forgotten how much each of you loves me. "Thank you" seems like a response too small for such great gestures. I am indebted to so many for their prayers, encouragements, calls and notes. You continue to restore life within me.

The last chapter of the book of my life has yet to be written.

Dan without Sandy

The Secret

———◆———

Dear Friends,

Many of you are aware that I suffer from osteo-arthritis and have limited mobility. I have been carrying a kidney stone in my right kidney for more than six months. With my chemotherapy and Sandy's passing away, some of you are wondering how I manage. I know this because a few of you have been brave enough to ask me, "What is your secret? What is keeping you from falling apart?" So, I will give you my secret (if you can call it that). It centers on my relationship with Sandy.

If I could speak the language of women and say the things that touch their hearts, or if I could express myself in words that women understand and use the vocabulary that seems to belong only to them, yet I never told Sandy how much I love her, my voice would be nothing more than wind blowing across my lips.

If somehow I could continue my conversations with Sandy now that she is gone, in the language of heavenly beings, but never told her how much she is loved, my voice would be little more than noise that is lost in a world of noise.

If I had the ability to see into the future and explain why cancer is, and why it destroys lives that are beautiful, productive and meaningful, but never said "I love you, honey," I would be little more than a fortune-teller, a tea-leaf reader, or a tarot-card interpreter.

If I could identify all of the barriers (some that became mountains) that have kept us apart when we should have been open, honest and together, and if I could also make them all disappear, but never really loved Sandy, my insights and skill would have been wasted, and Sandy and I would have gained nothing.

I am trying to say that there is a kind of love that is worth our investment. It is not found on TV or in the movies, and it is not something you "fall into." There is also a way to know whether or not you have this kind of love.

Whenever you want to give up and throw in the towel and call it quits, it is love that is patient and keeps on working. When unkind thoughts fill your head and some of them even spill out of your lips, it is love that is kind. This love reminds you that the object of your affection is more important than your opinion or your feelings and more important even than yourself.

This kind of love is not competitive—for in competition there is a loser as well as a winner. This love does not boast of achievements or brag of status. This love is never too proud to say, "I'm sorry." This love seeks to mend the fabric of relationships torn by selfish gestures.

This love is not rude or selfish or self-seeking, making one person small or insignificant in order to inflate the importance of another. Neither is this love easily angered. Notice I didn't say, "never gets angry." Before the sun goes down and the head hits the pillow at night, this love is in the process of reconciliation, rebuilding what was lost.

This love does not keep records of old hurts, opening wounds so they can never heal. Each day begins with a new slate. Each newly spoken "I love you" becomes as fresh and as meaningful as the first time it was spoken.

The love I have described protects each person and the relationship, hopes with a common heart about the future and keeps on keeping on.

God gave Sandy and me some wonderful tools to ensure a life together filled with joy. These tools are faith, hope and love. Take it from one who has used them all; love is the greatest—and endures even in death and beyond.

Dan

Alone

DEAR FRIENDS,

When an earthquake, floods or any natural disaster strikes it becomes a widely circulated news item. It remains in the news a few days until a new disaster moves to the front of our social awareness. Yet the results of each disaster, and the lingering effect it has, remain as elements that reshape lives. We withdraw our attention, and every person affected is left alone—alone in their pain, alone in their sorrow and alone in their loss. Each day brings new challenges.

Though I expected the loneliness to come, I didn't expect to be surprised and caught off guard by its arrival. I woke one morning and rolled over in bed and was shocked to find myself alone. For that moment I had forgotten that Sandy died. I was alone, very alone, and I was scared. The things I had read, the classes I had taken and the advice I had received had not prepared me for these moments of surprise.

On another occasion I woke and made my way to the kitchen to start the coffee. It is my habit to fix coffee first thing in the morning. For more than twenty years I fixed a cup of coffee with artificial cream for Sandy and took it to her as my morning expression of love. Some days she was in the shower. Some days she was getting dressed. Some days she was still in bed and woke to the new day with my offering of love. On this day, however, I opened the cabinet to get the cup and reached for the artificial cream. My hand froze in the air as if time had stopped. I had forgotten I would no longer be making that second cup of coffee. A door slammed shut in my face. Death had stolen my morning ritual. The pain of being alone washed over me afresh.

During the month before Christmas I received many cards. I opened each one and placed it in a pile on the dining table. The pile became very large. In mid-December I entered the room and caught a glimpse of that pile of Christmas cards and I realized that I had not sent out one card. "But," I reasoned with myself, "I have never sent out cards. Sandy did that." There were many places in our life together that were her territory, her space, her domain. I liked it that way. But now that space had no one in it. The tasks she had managed so well in our partnership were void. To be alone took on a new meaning. I began to realize that I must do the things I had always done before, and that I must now also do the things that she had done.

Those little surprises were like fresh tears in the wounds of emptiness. There were places in my life that only she could fill. Writing these chronicles helped me to cope with the loneliness of each day. Many of my writing moments were interrupted with sobbing as I relived the steps we walked together to the end of life.

It would be unfortunate indeed if I were to stop here and not share the impact that these notes have had on people around the world. Because of the computer and electronic mail, those first two hundred or so messages quickly became thousands. They were passed from parents to college children and from husband to wife, shared within prayer groups, used as the basis for sermons and sent to encourage others who struggle with cancer. When Sandy and I allowed our lives to be transparent through this most difficult journey, I never dreamed that our choice would result in such a powerful tool for others.

Permit me to paraphrase just some of the hundreds of responses I have received during this process.

One paralegal wrote to say that when she read the note called "Take My Hand," her head fell to her desk and she sobbed. When she recovered, she copied the note for everyone in her office. By the end of the day, a coworker who was getting married the next day asked permission to include these thoughts in her wedding vows.

A mother of a college student decided to send a series of these notes to her son who was away at school. She wrote to him, "You are old enough to know about life and death. Read these and please respond." When he had time to read the notes and absorb the messages, he wrote back to say that his life was changing. Things were becoming clearer.

Another woman wrote to say that she could not sleep and got up to read her e-mail. There she found a note from me. She was so convicted about her own marriage that when she went back to bed she reached for her husband's hand and held it tightly in hopes of communicating the love that I spoke about in my note.

One pastor wrote to say that he had been trying to preach for years about the principles contained in these notes. He was convinced that they were just words until they were practiced by people. He posted each note with a reference to how faith and love work to bring a person through crisis.

If I were to quote the apostle James in the first chapter of his book, he would say that I should count this experience as joy because of what it produced in me and in others. However, though I am aware of the changes in me, and the effect they have had on others, I am still left with an emptiness that will take time to heal. To help with that, I will fulfill a promise Sandy and I made to each other long ago. That promise was that whoever survived would throw a party to celebrate the life lived by the one who was gone.

Let the party begin and the joy return!

Dan